All the Air We Will Ever Breathe

poems by

Ruth Cassel Hoffman

Finishing Line Press
Georgetown, Kentucky

All the Air We Will Ever Breathe

To Miles, with love

Copyright © 2019 by Ruth Cassel Hoffman
ISBN 978-1-64662-091-3 First Edition
All rights reserved under International and Pan-American Copyright Conventions. No part of this book may be reproduced in any manner whatsoever without written permission from the publisher, except in the case of brief quotations embodied in critical articles and reviews.

ACKNOWLEDGMENTS

"The Bee Killers" was previously published as "The Closet" in a slightly different form, in *Poetry Northwest*, Volume XXVI, Number 3.
"Things She Had Always Believed In" was previously published as "A Form of Survival" in *The Seattle Review*, Volume IX, Number 2.
"In the Wyck Garden" was previously published in *Plainsongs*, Volume 11, Number 2.
"Uncloaked" (previously titled "Reading Poems") and "Rue du Cherche-Midi" (the latter in a slightly different form) were previously published in *Plainsongs*, Volume 11, Number 3.

Publisher: Leah Maines
Editor: Christen Kincaid
Cover Art: David O. Hearne
Author Photo: David O. Hearne
Cover Design: Elizabeth Maines McCleavy

Printed in the USA on acid-free paper.
Order online: www.finishinglinepress.com
also available on amazon.com

Author inquiries and mail orders:
Finishing Line Press
P. O. Box 1626
Georgetown, Kentucky 40324
U. S. A.

Table of Contents

No One Saw the Dog 1

Zydeco on the Radio 2

Gathering Daylight 3

Things She had Always Believed In 4

Uncloaked 5

All Night, Even the Corners Creep 6

Her Ex-Husband's Funeral 7

The Bee Killers 8

Doors 9

Before the Strawberry 10

Something We Need 11

How We Begin Again 12

In This State or Another 14

Dry Season 15

Gravity 16

The Woman Imagined a House 17

I Would Have Brought Tomatoes 18

White Horse Black Mountain, January 2017 19

Lightning Bugs 20

What Happened 21

Moving On 22

Days 23

Note for the Rat in My Pantry 24

Rue du Cherche-Midi 25

In the Wyck Garden 26

Ends 27

Atlantis 28

No One Saw the Dog

        —a streak of fox-red
across the green yard, a pounce.
Not I, and not the rabbit: just a kit,
too young to understand the exigencies
of life. Keep to the borders, watch your back.
The dog was there before the rabbit could slip
under the fence. What I saw was torn flesh,
hindquarters ripped open, pink ears flat
to grass. The last thing the bright black eye took in
was the broad blue uncompromising sky.
Was it a crow or a hawk that stole it?
The rabbit never knew. The dog came indoors,
nonchalantly we would say—

Zydeco on the Radio

Driving home past the Wild Goose Café
which I will never visit because
its name is more wonderful
than anything that could be inside,
finer than the thick-thin
green letters of its name,
driving past ditches inhabited
only by new snow and old ghosts
of purple joe-pye-weed, past
the thin black skin of the lake, driving
home from the poetry reading, saying only
yeah, yeah, et toi, to each thing
that passes, finding no way to paste
together the floating fragments
like ashes or scattered snow,
this unsubstantial juggling
with the spoons and thimbles
of everyday life, their very dailiness
a silence like dinner on the table,
no match for the jubilant
clatter and pump of this music.

Gathering Daylight

The rose-breasted grosbeak fans
his wings against the window
each spread feather backlit by cold sun
an instant before settling
on the dangling feeder.

Brush glistens not with snow, nor ice.
The twisted cherry tree silhouettes
itself in black. Sparrows
scatter on branches.

Time is light. Einstein
had it wrong—not energy.
Scientists say time
is slowing, will stop. Our star,
burnt out, light years from now.

I want to hoard this: creases of light
down High Windy, slant of sun
across Lenten rose, blue shadows on snow.

Things She Had Always Believed In

The weeping willow
dipping its limp froth in the river,
the white porch opening its lap to girls
in rockers and plump cats,
the sun draping floorboards
with white folds of warmth.
They lifted her from one age
to another, shored her up, spun her
in time until she reached this moment:
the rocker, the porch, the gray cat
all swept in sunlight, herself,
and out there the willow,
dipping, dipping. The secret
locked in her bent fingers,
in the rhythm of the floorboards
where she balances herself, impermanent
and necessary as air.

Uncloaked

André Breton, they say, read at Yale
    my wife with breasts of night
    tongue of amber and polished glass
while she smiled in the front row
and the students blushed.

Your poems embarrass me, says my son.
The only things my poems
strip are souls, his,
mine. His is cloaked—
a carapace whose underbelly
I have not found.

Mine is slivered moon, knife-
edge, light.

All Night, Even the Corners Creep

The browning plants
scowl at me from their dusty pots.
It's my fault. I am guilty.
Piles of mending watch me and sulk,
tug at secret holes. Mold grows
in mysterious jars, smirks
when I open the door. Someday
I will poison my family. Meantime
dust balls grow fat and lazy
in corners. Magazines whimper
when I add to the stack. I should feel sorry
and read them. Half-blind lamps
squint at me and snarl, "No reading here!"
The sky spies through the window, flings
snow at the pane. I will have to shovel—
plotting my escape.

Her Ex-Husband's Funeral
    for C.

I wasn't invited.
Sat in back, fled when they said
go in peace.

When he left, I stabbed
wildly with a kitchen knife,
bloodied my fingers.

I learned, slowly. His new wife
took his shirts to the cleaners.
My garden—poets' metaphor
for love—flourished. Weeds
moved to others' flower beds,
disturbing cozy domestic arrangements
among columbine and astilbe.

I gave speeches: how to make peace
with roses, how phlox changes
its colors, why prairie plants send
their roots deep into native soil. I know
what stays and what goes.

My daughters worry about me.
The old house has begun to wilt
and droop, my knees stiffen.
He left me twice.
Yet I stand.

The Bee Killers

Crawling under the eaves should
have been the hardest part.
My parents stripped the closet: books
of another age, suitcases, white
satin shoes. They shook honeybees
from silk-lined coffins
of handkerchiefs—a knothole, crack
in mortar must have let them in—
spaces between studs crammed
with honeycomb spilling over.
My parents pumped poison
into the walls. The china-headed doll
was lying in the last box, honey
dripping onto her bone teeth. My mother
combed the doll's hair, wiped
her curved wooden fingers clean.
That night, she dreamed of crushing
honeycomb onto her bread,
her tongue.

Doors

You wanted to pick up
your prescription

at Walmart, but the steel
curtain is locked.

The bank closed, the doctor
playing golf. Your friend has pinned a note

to the doorbell. Your life:
a puzzle-locked room.

But somewhere
a door opens.

An inch. Two.
A narrow wedge glimmers

the floorboards. Trickles
out, arranges itself like an alphabet

red and blue across the fridge
door, declaring itself

a poem. You had almost forgotten
what it feels like—

more refreshing than the cold
beer behind the door.

Before the Strawberry

How it comes to be night.
Whether the she-bear
wakens in her dim cave

when her cubs are born.
Where to find the ten
billion years since that first star

exploded into light.
Whether the wild creatures
know us as theirs. How

to measure the exact
peak of ripeness before
the strawberry decays.

What other words I might
shape with these letters.
What sound they will make

when it comes to be night.
Why we are strangers.
How we cling to this earth

and why. What the earth
claims of each of us.
Whether we will waken.

.

Something We Need

i. The Doe

Our first lesson: withhold
breath, those small puffs
of steam that give away
the life in us. Next, raise
our eyes to see her, the color
of November grasses, her eyes
glistening in morning sun. Then
stillness, a way to etch this beauty
on all the air we will ever
breathe.

ii. The Marsh

What do dumb creatures know
of hope, ranging for tender
shoots in a winter-stripped
world? They sleep
with one eye open, drink
the rain—an armor
of stillness upon them.

iii. How We Go On

How will we learn to trust
the wrinkled earth, the open
eye of the sun, the milkweed pod
exploding into air?
Those winged seeds settling
on the marsh pond, a mist
we could touch—something we need
bears them up.
We wait for some green
thing in this brown world.

How We Begin Again
for Enzo

In my friend's dream, he flies out
over the cliff. He balances
on logs in the woods, sinks

below water. He doesn't
wake up. *I have to paint,* he says.
I'm going to start painting again.

His dreams are of water, diving
as deep as a house in the dark.
I'm not afraid of anything
when I'm awake. I imagine

what he will paint: Something the color
of frosted plums reaches off the canvas,
and the corners are green: living,

but small, and behind it all, a dark wing,
black edges feathering. His painting
is in a secret room in someone else's house.

How will he keep the dark from closing in?
He forgets how to stop:
a small death, each time.

We talk about shapes, on the page,
in the stone. Michelangelo
finished *minuziosamente*

his Rondini Pietà, but left an arm
disjointed, rough, belonging
to another life in the stone.

I can't go back, he says. *Someone else
did those paintings.* His hands draw
new shapes in his white kitchen, dark

pools in the forest and waves against
the cliff. Like writing the same poem
over and over, looking
for the one true shape of the wave.

In This State or Another

a boy picks up his AR-15 and takes it
to school. Sun glints on the barrel
just before he steps inside
and shoots seventeen people,
or twelve, or twenty. One, a boy
who will never bring his favorite yellow
Matchbox car to school again.

In a city where heat rises
from concrete as from yellow sand,
a man picks up a stone and aims it
at his wife, the wife he loved until
she said she wanted to study.
She fixes bright sun with her eyes
so she will not see the stone.

Another wife forgets to buy
crackers. She buckles when the fist
smashes her ribs. Her lungs
empty as she folds into the sunny
patch on the kitchen floor.

On a sunny day—it will be sunny,
but first light has just crept around
the blackout shades—it seems gray
because we've seen it over and over
on grainy film—men with pistols rouse
whole families and march
them through streets. Trains are waiting;
they must hurry.

On a sunny day, a Northern flicker invades
my backyard. That slash of red about the eye.
A flash of yellow at the tail, like sunlight,
when he startles and flies.

Dry Season

That was no farm my grandparents bought—
30 acres of foot-tall grass, scrubby
red cedar, a creek that ran nowhere
in spring and not at all in summer.
The well was contaminated,
barn ready to fold in on itself,
home to owls and one rusted Model T.

We bounced in that truck
through uncut fields,
bumper shearing off daisies
and Queen Anne's lace, tossing them
like rain into summer air—

how some people live:
flinging poems on the page
as if words grew wild

like blue flag iris.
Sunlight flashes among trees,
blooming everywhere.

Gravity

The sky is silver, translucent.
Overhead, a blurred airliner dreams
from right to left above a thin wash of gray.

Who could believe
in the airplane, despite grade-school
displays on the Bernoulli principle?

We're dealing in sheer impossibilities.
How we stand with our two feet
on this earth we believe to be solid enough

to hold us up (though once we thought
we could dig to China, in the sand under
the back shed, beside the rusty red tricycle).

How our bodies remember—brush of leaf,
pressure of wind—that *tree*
is beautiful, a *tornado* is terrible.

We fold into ourselves
at the very thought *we may lose ourselves
in this wash and wind.* How the sky shows

its true colors. How a plane,
everything unholy, sometimes breaks
through. We are skating

on thin earth. Trees fall, hearts
split apart. The angels crashed through
centuries ago. We believe in *maybe,
close your eyes, I will never fall.*

The Woman Imagined a House

so full she wept in every room.
She dreamed her husband's first wife
was insane. On the frames of photographs
she met the ex-wife's fingers.
Her husband embraced her:
You are *my first wife.* He opened
his hands and smiled.

Before that, she found stones
in her pockets, knives at hand
every day. She saw dead
gardens in the park, scarred
like a grave strewn with pebbles.
The days were long: her hands
folded themselves together
like the covers of a book.

Once she believed that somewhere
a prairie fire flung ashes
against the sky. Her husband said,
Give me the matches. She said,
They are gone. The days were long:
she no longer read the books
on the table. The photographs
kept their backs to the wall.

When she left her husband,
she flew night after night over the park;
she flew beneath the bleached soil
where crocus bulbs curled
in the dark. *Come back,*
he called, *tell me where
you have been*—but his voice
looped a thin thread
across the sky to the other side.

I Would Have Brought Tomatoes
for W. Morris Cassel, 1912-2006

In my garden, a green so lush
I think I'm back in rainforest.
Tomatoes lean into each other,
heavy, pale globes, each
bearing future sweetness:
purple, gold, maroon, zebra-striped.

My father leaned into my mother.
She cradled his hand
as if by holding on
she could let go. His breath
faltered. We waited.

He taught us to do things right,
to repair what can be repaired,
to think, trust science, not
miracles. I'm the daughter
who mislearned every lesson.
Dying is mostly waiting.

I plant tomatoes, prowl
daily in my jungle, search
for reds and golds.
Small green tomatoes fall
into my hand; unsorted photos
lie askew on tables. Sometimes
I can order the world.

His last lesson: how to go when it is time.
He released his last breath.
I would have brought tomatoes,
but I can't speed ripening.
Instead I bring him words
he can't hear, spread out on warm air.

White Horse Black Mountain, January 2017

Roy "Future Man" Wooten and master kalimba player Kevin Spears
are dueling it out on stage. Their fingers fly over instruments
I've never seen before: red drum with a neck like a banjo,
silver space saucer that plays melodies, digital digeridoo
shaped like a cigar box. The music bounces off chairs and walls.
Kevin and Roy face each other, daring one another
to play faster, syncopate rhythms, keep up.

Future Man won't stop. He plunges headlong:
everything improvised, like yesterday
and tomorrow. Will I press the accelerator
instead of the brake, trip on the top step?
I need to know the unknowable.

Overhead artificial stars twinkle and spin
on black ceiling, fling up sparks, so I think: fire.
The music drives forward, lifts me out of my chair.
I walk out into cold night, button
my coat of jazz with notes spilling
from its pockets.

Lightning Bugs

a firestorm of *flash flash*
zigzagged across our postage-stamp backyard
where hot twilight bloomed
around our shorts-clad churning legs
empty jars in one hand
punctured lids in the other
shouting *I got one!* and *Look!*
until we trooped upstairs to bed
flash
flash

flash

and we slept,
and they slept
the sleep of the dead.

What Happened

It is possible that—
in a Norwegian cabin
in a grassy sheep meadow
on a mountain slope,
a broad September sky
laid out before us
in the wall-sized picture window,
after making love
in the top bunk—
I slid to the floor, naked, arms raised,
jubilant, breasts and belly washed
in afternoon sun
for a pair of American tourists
backing away from the glass.

Moving On

Today you caught me
        talking to those black
clouds, and you
        said *Complaining*
won't make them go
        away, just move
on, and I said *Wait,*
        wait, and this evening

the moon was tangled
        in black branches.
The clouds had moved on,
        hiding someone else's
moon, and I said *I*
        want that silver
platter, and you said
        It is knotted

in the trees. Someone
        else is waiting for it,
and I said *If I walk*
        far enough I will be
that person.

Days

Today a watery sun warms fresh mulch on the bank by the stream.

*

My coffeemaker sighs and babbles in the corner, indecipherable as birdsong.

*

Birdsong a tensile fabric draped over dogwood and cherry. Grass rife with clover.

*

Waking, I'm a stone in warm earth. Afternoons, a lavender crocus in a crowd of grass.

*

Evenings, an ember. Ash below me, smoke rising.

*

I sit on the back porch, watch how the wren's beak trembles when it sings. How leaves twist on their stems just before rain.

*

What I knew yesterday, I no longer know.

Note for the Rat in My Pantry

I heard your music. For nights,
your teeth played percussion in my walls,
bringing the house down
with crescendos of gnawed joists.
I can't sleep through your concert.
I was awake when you crept into my pantry,
carrying your fat fur on your back
and twitching your tail.
I reached for broom and rake,
an old paint can; closed the doors.
Those animal snarls I heard were not yours;
I clutched my weapon like a soul.

It was the flashlight that got you. You clung
to its beam. I dragged you out
from under the fridge,
flopping like an ash-gray fish,
the fireplace tongs squeezing
your soft belly.
The last I saw of you,
you were drowning
in an inch
of white paint.

But you'll be back:
haunting my house is your business.
You'll be ants on my table,
beetles scuttling into my fireplace.

You'll be the invisible spores
that float in my air, settle on my bread.
I'll be watching for you:
We have unfinished business, you and I.

Rue du Cherche-Midi
for Greg, now a man

You would want it to happen
in a Paris café: the stone façades,
the faceless floating skirts and shoes

bustling, a glass of wine on the table.
All clichés, and you a cliché as well:
a boy, wanting to be a man, wanting

to meet Hemingway. What if he sat across
from you in the bentwood chair?
Would you push the glass to him,

smile, ask about the sea? If you
bent your broad-brimmed hat towards him,
leaned out of your too-thin reality,

a sudden constellation: yellow wine
spinning stars on the gleaming black
tabletop, the old man: a supernova—

light gone out, still pulsing
in the afternoon sky—and you,
peeling time like an orange,

flinging aside hours and datelines,
looking for that hot bright noon
at the beginning of desire.

In the Wyck Garden

The green has already gone
from the garden. We have forgotten
the colors of the flowers. Summer
night floats down from the tower,
scatters the bells. The round Dutch tones
roll down, full-breasted pigeons
folding their gray wings. Roses
settle onto their stems in the shadows,
the bells onto our hands.
We'll carry them home like petals.
The garden has been here for centuries,
waiting for this moment: we sit blooming
in the gray garden, as if the moments
were not deepening from moth to swift
to dusky bat, a dark breeze
alongside our cheeks, and gone.

Ends

The future afghan lies in my lap,
a heap of yellow yarn tangled
as the lives of characters on TV.

You have quick hands, my mother said.
Quickness is no advantage
dealing with yarn. Untangling
is the price you pay. Making,
unmaking—slow work.

Like that walk in the woods, loop
after loop, where we could not see
the end of the trail.

When her husband
died, our friend said *He wasn't afraid
to die. He just wasn't done living.*

Atlantis

Imagine
all the fish in the sea
trailing streams of phosphorescence
in their wake, weaving
highways the color
of neon lights waiting
for their cities to be built.

And I could ride those highways
to the bottom of the world,
slide hand over hand until
my fingers grew fins
and my red lungs slept.

No more pressing my face
into the wind, lifting
blind feet, moving my body
from the path of trees.
I'd slice
through water
like a silver knife, my eyes
glowing blue in the dark.

Thank you...

I have been writing poems for some forty years, but this is my first chapbook. Slow learner, I guess. How can I possibly thank all the people who have helped to make this happen?

To my poetry group in South Bend, Indiana, 1970s and 1980s: Sonia Gernes, Joan McIntosh, Julie Herrick White, Max Westler, and the late Ernest Sandeen, all of whom helped me transition from writing in French to writing in English, and who first taught me how to polish my work;

To my poetry group in Black Mountain, NC, since 2016: Norma Bradley, Janet Ford, Kathy Nelson, Jeanette Reid, Mike Ross, Bruce Spang, and Alida Woods, whose encouragement is always as deep as their astute critiques, and whose love is invaluable;

To Tina Barr, in whose workshops I learned to disconnect from the poem I thought was done, and to turn a dispassionate eye on every letter and every comma;

To Shaindel Beers, friend and poet, who has never stopped supporting my efforts and whose careful editing helped the final shaping of each of these poems, and to Jenn Givhan, whose laser-like focus made me rethink the lines I was most in love with;

To the editors who have turned down my work, teaching me humility and persistence;

To my parents, Charlotte McKelvey Cassel and W. Morris Cassel, who never said "you can't do that", and to my siblings, brother Bill Cassel and his amazing wife Boots and sister Jean Campbell and her amazing husband Bruce, all a deep and constant source of encouragement, love, and support;

And finally, to my husband, Miles Hoffman, who is my *sine quo non*—my "without whom not"—my partner and my love,

Thank you.

Ruth Cassel Hoffman grew up in Philadelphia and spent many years living in flatland (alias the Midwest). Always a lover of words, she majored in French in college, earned her Ph.D. at the University of Chicago in medieval French literature, and spent ten years teaching French at St. Mary's College and Indiana University at South Bend. She developed and managed programs funded by the Indiana Committee for the Humanities, including one—*Poetry in the Palm of Your Hand*—that brought together poets and the deaf community, and featured poetry in American Sign Language. She worked as a freelance writer for a time until she founded Language Resources Ltd., which provided foreign language training for corporate clients and others.

Ruth and her husband Miles relocated to Chicago, where she expanded Language Resources. A highlight of that period was helping to design a program through the Northern Illinois Conference of the United Methodist Church, to teach basic Spanish to congregations in order to live radical hospitality among their Spanish-speaking neighbors. The book that Ruth co-wrote for that project—*Who Is My Neighbor? ¿Quién Es Mi Vecino? Learning Spanish as Church Hospitality*—is available through Cokesbury Press.

She and her husband then adopted the town of Black Mountain, NC, where they can stand in front of their house and see tall trees and ancient mountains on all sides, share their backyard with the occasional black bear and constant birdsong, and don't have to shiver in the Chicago winters. Knitting and crocheting, learning to play the mountain dulcimer, and of course writing poetry fill her days.

Ruth wrote her first "adult" poem (beyond childhood scribblings) in French while driving 60 miles an hour on the Chicago Skyway, one hand on the wheel and a pen in the other. It was nearly illegible, but she loved the danger of it. Years later, she sticks to English, which is after all her native language, though that doesn't make the crafting of a poem any easier. She is not one of those poets whose pens leak poems just lying on the desk; she has to scrabble in the dirt for them. Her poems have been published in *The Seattle Review, Plainsongs, Poetry Northwest, Yankee Magazine* and *Rattle*. She loves how poems tell you what you didn't know yet.

www.ingramcontent.com/pod-product-compliance
Lightning Source LLC
LaVergne TN
LVHW041510070426
835507LV00012B/1468